THE WORLD'S TENNIS BOOK EVER

Rod Newcombe's
THE WORLD'S BEST
TENNIS
BOOK EVER

Limited Edition No. _____ / 1,000,000

Other books in this series
The World's Best Running Book ever
The World's Best Cricket Book ever
The World's Best Golf Book ever
The World's Best Horseracing Book ever
The World's Best Rugby Book ever

CREDITS

Written by Peter Sherwood and Gary Alderdice
Graphic design and drawings by Roy Bisson
Editor, Peter Sherwood
Mr. Rosewall's hairdressing by Brylcreem
Typeset in Australia by Sunshine
Enquiries, writs and donations should be addressed to:
Lincoln Green Publishing, 19th floor, Tai Sang
Commercial Building, 24 Hennessy Road, Hong Kong.

© Lincoln Green Publishing

ISBN 962 7028 09 6

'If you know how to return my shots with a speedy left hand, I am yours. You do not? Then give up the ball, you awkward clown . . .'

Martial, Roman Poet, 40-104 AD
Patti McGuire to Jimmy Connors 1978

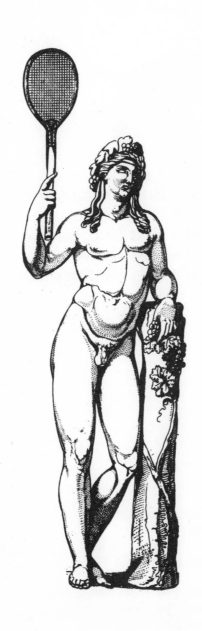

Contents

Publisher's Note

Thanks to a recent innovation in graphic design page numbers are not being used in this book. Instead, a revolutionary new method employing letters of the alphabet will guide you from subject to subject with remarkable ease.

Beginning with the letter 'A' (formerly page 1) just follow the letters in alphabetical order through 'B' (page 2), 'C' (page 3), 'D' (page 4) and so on, until you reach the letter 'Z' which is what used to be page 26.

Then, you simply start again (ABC etc.). The publishers hope that this simplified method (the patent of a leading Dublin designer) gives you many hours of pleasurable reading.

Foreword

A lot of people might think that the biggest thrill of my life was to have won the Men's Singles at Wimbledon five times in a row but really you know that it wasn't and neither was my winning the French Championship six times or the Davis Cup single-handed I have to say that neither has there been any feeling of excitement in winning the Masters I forget how many times and I've always been too bored with the US open to play any good tennis although the planes taking off help to keep you awake but when the publishers of this book asked me to write the foreword I wasn't interested at all and then they offered me some money and Mr McCormack got very excited on my behalf I hope you find my foreword interesting and maybe even a little bit amusing perhaps.

Bjorn Borg

Penny, Pin-ching & Wong

Solicitors and Notaries Public
Hong Kong

28th August 1980

To the Joint Authors, The World's Best Tennis Book Ever.

Dear Sirs,

Further to our recent discussions on the manuscript submitted by you for our advice on possible infringement of both civil and criminal laws of libel we confirm and wish to record in the strongest possible terms our verbal advices to you of the 23rd ultimo that publication of the text, illustrations and captioned photographs would inevitably give rise to immediate injunctions restraining distribution.

Such initial judicial intervention would certainly be followed by writs for substantial and punitive damages against you.

We have sought counsels advice as requested and the opinion of Sir Evelyn Bottomry-Bond Q.C. is detailed below:

> 'Matter is essentially defamatory if it tends to blacken the character of another and thereby to expose him to public hatred contempt and ridicule; it is that which traduces or vilifies the subject and tends to arise angry passions endangering public peace. It is sufficient if the text or illustrations set the subject in a discreditable, scurrilous ignominious or ludicrous light. Scandals published of a body of men are also within cognizance of the law.

> 'Some passages in the text are little more than disgraceful and opprobrious libel against some of the most generous, talented and distinguished sporting and administrative figures in the tennis world. Viewed objectively the manuscript is not only offensive but is obviously calculated to denigrate and draw into disrepute and public contempt officials, players and institutions alike in a sport which has become steeped in dignity down through the ages.'

We feel bound to further inform you that publication in the face of this advice, would aggravate the quantum of damages awarded against you.

We trust that wise counsel will prevail and enclose a note of our professional charges. Kindly arrange settlement thereof before publication of the material, should you elect to ignore our advice.

Yours faithfully,

Ben T. Penny

THE ABC OF TENNIS

A

Amritraj, Vijay
Disqualified from Poona Open 1963 for trying to curry favour with officials.

Amritraj, Anand
Brother of Vijay and Ashok

Amritraj, Ashok
Brother of Anand and Vijay

Amritraj, Mrs.
Mother of Amritraj brothers

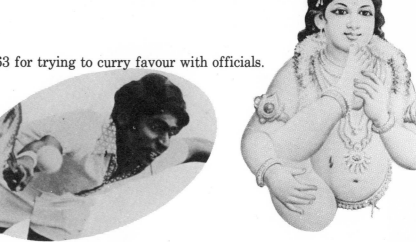

Advantage
What members of the royal family have in getting tickets to Wimbledon.

Ambidextrous
Renee Richards

Do you think the courts will dry by 3 o'clock Vijay?

Alley

(USA) area of Court bounded by singles sideline and doubles sideline. Used in doubles, also for qualifiers without hotel accommodation. Tramlines (Aust) — more hazardous for sleeping in.

Angle-game

Style of play where the ball is hit so as to force the opponent wide of court. Can also involve very low shots which are played off the angles or towards the end of legs.

Amateur

A player who is identifiable by his repeated assertions that he receives no financial assistance from any source whatsoever. Virtually extinct.

Australia

Fifty and more years ago players would travel months by ship to go there to play a few sets in the Davis Cup. This cultural nirvana is now considered too far away even for Australian players, most of whom live in the US.

Australian Championships

Once the sole property of Roy Emerson who, in a gesture of pure benevolence, returned them to the ATA during his farewell speech in the bar at Sydney's Kingsford Smith Airport, shortly before being assisted onto a Qantas flight to Los Angeles.

Backhand
Invented by K. Rosewall in the middle of the 19th century. Original still in use.

Ball
Held the night of the Wimbledon singles final.

Balls
More than one ball.

Borg
Grob spelled backwards. Generally accepted as Scandinavian origin.

Black
Arthur Ashe. Won Wimbledon. Speared to death while on a peace mission in Johannesburg.

Ballboys
Group of small children paid by players to distract opponents.

Beer
Basis of the Australian junior training programme.

Baseline
Two inch wide mark at the rear of the court. Said to contain hypnotic qualities giving double vision to players and umpires.

Bjorn Borg
This player has captivated Wimbledon crowds with his extroverted antics during match play. Proof that top players are Bjorn not made.

French tennis officials are apprehended by police as they're about to leave Rolland Garros Stadium in 1932 after stealing the Davis Cup from America.

Borota, Jean

One of the French Four Musketeers with Cochet, LaCoste and Brugnan. A flamboyant and athletic player, the Bounding Basque spearheaded the partisan French defence of the Davis Cup in 1932 when aided by a well watered clay court and bad linecalls the French managed to retain the coveted prize.

ABOUT THE AUTHORS

Both the authors come from the antipodes, a quaint English term for Australia and New Zealand. These two countries first gained the attention of the world when it was discovered that bath water there went down the plughole in the opposite direction to bathwater in the more northern countries. Little has happened in Australia or New Zealand since.

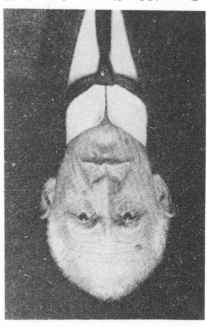

Gary Alderdice was born in New Zealand. Despite this he pressed on to become a criminal lawyer. He was quickly caught and served six years in Wellington before being invited to join Her Majesty's Government in Hong Kong as a Crown Counsel. Married with four children he is seldom off the tennis court and was last seen by his wife during typhoon Ted, August 26th, 1977. He was practicing his backhand in the bathroom.

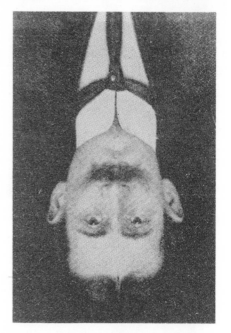

Peter Sherwood began playing tennis in Sydney at the age of nine. Following six years of extensive training under the guidance of Dinny Pails and later Harry Hopman, he was sent overseas at the expense of the Australian Association of Tennis Coaches; first to Ootacumund in Southern India and then to Cochabamba in Bolivia. He is presently continuing lessons in Hong Kong.

The only known photograph of the Crutchlow wedding. Twenty years later the couple's widely differing political opinions would bring about separation and ultimately divorce. Mrs Crutchlow was 8' 4"

Court, Margaret
Australia's greatest-ever woman player. Became so famous that the playing surface was named after her.

Crutchlow, Bartholomew
At 3' 6" was believed to be the world's smallest tennis player. Born in Maccelsfield, England 1815 Crutchlow's incredibly fast service once defeated a racehorse at Epsom when it hit the feeding animal in the ear. He was unbeaten until 1856 when the net was introduced into tournament play. Left his mark indelibly on the game by recording the highest number of bruised and broken ankles in history. He is buried just behind the new changing rooms at the Limpsfield Memorial Hockey and Tennis Club.

MANY FACES OF A CHAMPION

The tension and excitement of tournament play takes a heavy emotional toll on every player on the circuit. When you're number one the strain of staying at the top can be almost overwhelming. Relaxing between matches is also a vital part of winning. It's a life of ups and downs.

At a recent European event our photographer captured the many moods of Bjorn Borg.

1. . . . 'that was a yard in!'

2. . . . philosophical

3. . . . the joy of victory

4. . . . the agony of defeat

5. . . . confident, smiling . . . a winner

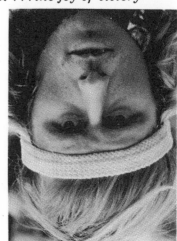

6. . . . 'concentrate!!'

7. . . . eye on the ball

8. . . . sharing a joke with the crowd

Choke

Colloquial (slang) term for state of extreme nervousness. To tighten up in the game, to lose rhythm. Can lead to the player losing his advantage and usually the match. This phenomenon has been known to affect linesmen who make adverse calls, and umpires who confirm them.

Crosscourt

Shot hit from one side of the court to the diagonally opposite side designed to make opponent move. Has the advantage of passing over the middle and lowest part of the net in flight. Some tall players impart topspin to this shot giving rise to the ball and to the term "highballs".

Crowd

Thousands of ordinary people paying dearly to sit close together and move their heads from side to side in unison during a tennis match.

Cawley

Roger. Husband of Evonne Goolagong and sometime mentor. Receives room and board for sending cigarette smoke signals to his wife during her matches.

Connors, Jimmy *Homme d'es prit*
Humorist and wit who made the big time as a tennis player. Of only minor importance as a comic performer.

Cox, Mark
Rhymes with lox. (See under bagels and Harold Solomon.)

Caravaggio, Michelangelo Merisi
Italian painter and sportsman of the 17th century. On May 29th, 1606 he killed his opponent Ranuccio Tomasoni in a *rachetta* match at Muro Torto after a violent quarrel over the awarding of a point. There is little chance of such an unsportsmanlike gesture occurring today, racquets being so much lighter.

THIS BOOK
WILL BE SENT TO ANY ADDRESS
FREE
BY MAIL POSTPAID ON APPLICATION

WRITE A LETTER OR A POSTAL CARD

AND SAY

END ME YOUR BIG CATALOGUE

.l it will be sent to you im-
.nediately free by mail, postpaid.

WRITE A LETTE OR A POSTAL CAR

AND SAY

SEND ME YOU BIG CATALOGU

and it will be sent to you ir
mediately free by mail, postpai

SIMPLE RULES FOR ORDERING.

USE OUR ORDER BLANK IF YOU HAVE ONE. If you haven't one, use any plain paper.

TELL US IN YOUR OWN WAY WHAT YOU WANT, always giving the CATALOGUE NUMBER of each article
.d be sure to state size and color where required. Enclose in the letter the amount of money, either a postoffice money order
which you get at the postoffice, an express money order, which you get at the express office, or a draft, which you ge
at any bank; or put the money in the letter, take it to the postoffice and tell the postmaster you want it registere

IF YOU LIVE ON A RURAL MAIL ROUTE, just give the letter and the money to the mail carrier and he will get th
money order at the postoffice and mail it in the letter for you.

DON'T BE AFRAID YOU WILL MAKE A MISTAKE. We receive hundreds of orders every day from young an
old who never before sent away for goods. We are accustomed to handling all kinds of orders.

TELL US WHAT YOU WANT IN YOUR OWN WAY, written in any language, no matter whether good or po
writing, and the goods will be promptly sent to you.

WE HAVE TRANSLATORS TO READ AND WRITE ALL LANGUAGES.

DON'T BE AFRAID OF THE FREIGHT OR EXPRESS CHARGES. You must pay them when you get th
goods at the station, but they never amount to much compared with what we save you in cost.

IF YOU FIND IT NECESSARY TO HAVE SOME SPECIAL INFORMATION you can undoubtedly obtain it b
.ferring to the matter contained within the first twelve pages of this catalogue.

ENKLA REGLER ATT IAKTTAGA VID BESTÄLLNING.

Begagna vår beställningsblankett, om ni har en sådan.
Om icke, begagna vanligt rent papper.

Säg oss på edert eget sätt hvad ni önskar, alltid uppgif-
de katalognumret på hvarje sak. Inneslut beloppet i
.vet antingen i postoffice money order, hvilken köpes å
.stkontoret; express money order, hvilken köpes å express-
.ntoret, eller en vexel, hvilken kan köpas å hvilken bank
.n helst, eller också inneslut kontanta penningar i brefvet,
.g det till postkontoret och säg postmästaren att ni önskar
.a det registrerat.

Var icke rädd för att ni gör ett misstag. Vi erhålla hun-
.atals beställningar dagligen från unga och gamla hvilka
.rig förr sändt efter varor. Vi äro vana vid att expediera
.a slags beställningar.

Säg oss på edert eget sätt hvad ni önskar. Skrif på hvil-
.et språk som helst, bra eller dålig stafning, bra eller dålig
.andstil, och varorna skola blifva eder prompt tillsända.

Vi ha öfversättare som läsa och skrifva alla språk.

Det är icke nödvändigt för eder att genomläsa de första
.o sidorna i denna katalog, såvida ni icke önskar någon spe-
.ell upplysning. Dessa tio sidor innehålla detaljerad upp-
.ysning, så att de som i alla delar önska göra sig förtrogna
.ä sättet att beställa och sända varor, fraktkostnader o. s. v.,
.s.y., icke behöfva skrifva till oss, utan helt enkelt kunna
.ä upp dessa sidor och finna den upplysning de önska.

Einfache Regeln zum Bestellen.

Gebraucht unsere Bestellungszettel wenn Sie welche haben, we
nicht nehmen Sie gewöhnliches Papier.

Im Bestellen erwähnen Sie die Catalog Numero an alle
Sachen. Die Bestellung soll das Geld enthalten, entweder ein
„Postoffice Money Order," (welche man gewöhnlich an der Post be
kommen kann), eine "Expreß Money Order," ein Bank Certificat
das man an jeder Bank bekommen kann, oder legen Sie das Gel
in den Brief mit der Bestellung, in welchem Falle Sie den Bri
Eingeschrieben schicken sollten. Der Brief wird in der Po
Eingeschrieben (Registered.)

Wir erhalten jeden Tag eine große Anzahl von Bestellungen vo
allen Leuten (Jung und Alt).

Sie brauchen nicht furchtsam zu sein Sachen zu bestellen, wir we
den Ihr Bestellung schon verstehen.

Schreiben Sie uns in Ihrer eigener Weise, und in Ihrer eige
ner Sprache, was Sie wollen, einerlei ob gut oder schlecht geschrie
ben, und die Waare wird Ihnen sofort zugeschickt.

Wir haben Leute bie alle Sprachen schreiben und übersetzen.

Die ersten zehn Seiten in diesem Catalog beziehen sich hauptsäch
lich an die Frachtbetrage der verschiedenen Waare und hat nur Wich
tigkeit für Sie im Falle Sie in diesen Einzelheiten interessiert sind.

DO NOT FAIL TO GIVE SIZE, COLOR, WEIGHT, ETC., IF RE~comparably low price 'EN WRITING YOUR ORDER

Dipping Balls
Balls that barely clear the net, then drop fast and short. Most effective in damp conditions when balls are also termed "heavy". Players afflicted with either complaint should not attempt to vault the net after victory.

Dod, Charlotte
Youngest ever Wimbledon champion. At age 15 won Womens Singles in 1887 and again in 1888, 1891, 1892, 1893. Won British Open Golf Championship 1904. Semi finalist in 1889, 1899. Played Hockey for England v. Ireland 1899, 1900. Silver Medalist 1908 Olympics in Archery. Also distinguished skater, horserider, mountaineer and billiard player. Known as "the Little Wonder". Slept in her spare time. Died at age 91.

Double fault
Phenomena observed during play at San Andreas Open, San Francisco California, in 1906.

Dink
Taken between games by children to restore fluid balance.

Donnay
Little known brand of tennis racquet. Can be strung to over 80lbs, but impossible to play with.

Deuce
The French contribution to Lawn Tennis.

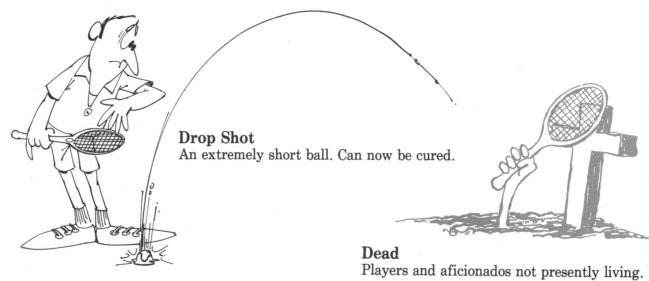

Drop Shot
An extremely short ball. Can now be cured.

Dead
Players and aficionados not presently living.

Davis Cup
Donated by Dwight W. Davis to Australia who returned it when it was found to be empty.

Marks hands Ashe shock defeat

Melbourne, Jan 2,
Unseeded Australian John Marks survived two match points on his way to a shock win over American Arthur Ashe in the semi-finals of the Australian Open tennis championships today.

Marks (26) defeated third seed Ashe 6-4, 6-2, 2-6, 1-6, 9-7 in a three hours 14 minutes marathon and now meets favourite Guillermo Vilas of Argentina for the title.

Vilas sped into the final with a merciless 6-2, 6-0, 6-3 triumph over young American Hank Pfister.

Marks' victory was a crushing blow to Ashe who needed to reach the final in order to qualify for the important Masters tournament in New York on January 10.

Marks, who let Ashe back into the match after winning the first two sets, was himself in danger of defeat when 4-5 and 15-40 down in a desperate decider.

Two spectacular passing shots saved him and Marks went on to end a sequence of six successive service breaks by both players to lead 8-7. He sealed the match with yet another break in the next game.

Ashe was convinced he had victory within his grasp after levelling at two-sets-all. "I have never lost a match being up 5-4, 40-15 in the third or fifth set," he said.

The American is now in ninth position, one outside the eight-player Masters line-up and can only play if someone drops out.

Australian Mark Edmondson, Marks' doubles partner, became the first unseeded player to win the Australian Open when he beat compatriot John Newcombe three years ago.

Marks said he sharpens up for matches by shooting starlings with an airgun every morning. Before facing Ashe, Marks put in some target practice and said: "That's my standard breakfast, a bowl of cornflakes and a couple of starlings."

Vilas needed only 90 minutes to tear Pfister apart and book his place in the final.

American Betsy Nagelsen, ranked 68th in the world, and Australian Chris O'Neill, 110th, contest the women's title.

If we hadn't had that curry last night it would have taken hours to inflate this thing.

GREAT MOMENTS IN TENNIS HISTORY
SERIES NO. 11

November 6 1979, and 6,000 people packed the Workers Stadium in Canton to see the World's No. 1 player Bjorn Borg play Australia's John Alexander. It was the first time a world tennis champion has played in China. Some of the enthusiastic press comments appear on page 90.

Excuses
Haven't played for weeks. Sore arm. Hangover. Bad light. Bad balls. Too hot. Too cold. The best excuses should precede the game. Any utterance after a loss is considered an excuse.

Elbow
Believed to be of Antipodean origin, the word describes a state of extreme nervous tension on a tight point when a player is afraid to hit the ball freely. Colloquially it is expressed as "...'e got the elbow at set point in the fifth".

Evert, Chris
Anne Jones said of her, "Virginia will have to come to the net if she's going to get back into this match..."

Edinburgh, Duke of
Originally Greek. Sometimes gets free tickets to Wimbledon. Occasionally presents the trophies. Secretly prefers Polo.

Evert-Lloyd, John
Husband of Chris.

Finger
Found in a group along the arm. Sometimes presented to linesmen or umpires. (see Nastase).

Forecourt
Area of court between service line and net. After service player should move to this area quickly to volley return.

Foreplay
Australian players are known to move quickly through this area before beginning service.

Footfault
Caused when end of server's leg slips into a crack in the court.

Flushing Meadow
Part of La Guardia Airport, New York. Used once a year for the U.S. Open.

Forest Hills
Site of supermarket and commercial complex.

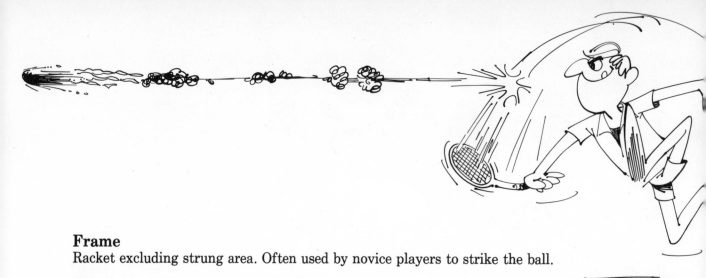

Frame
Racket excluding strung area. Often used by novice players to strike the ball.

Fastest Service
Lady Emily Montague of 'the Willows', Buckinghamshire was served with a bowl of strawberries and cream 9 minutes 48 seconds after paying £10 at Wimbledon on July 6th 1958. She received no change. Fastest measured service was struck in 1931 by William Tatem Tilden then aged 38. Ball speed was measured at 163.6 mph.

Flange, Nobby
Former English touring professional renowned for variety of grips used during matches, especially in humid climates. His motto "get a grip on it" sums up his attitude to the game. He favoured the traditional Eastern grip but had the uncanny ability to shift to a modified Continental under stress without losing rhythm. His dry wit and pithy humour were the hallmark of his play, as was his lisp. His use of the Continental grip when playing rising balls was intuitive. On Californian courts he would switch to the Western grip, usually ineffective against both tall players and high balls, and with his powerful wrist and elbow could still control most balls. Known to grip the shaft of the racket for maximum control. Never changed hands during a match.

Fault
Large crack in Californian tennis court.

Foro Italico
Tennis stadium in Rome. Built in 1935 under the direction of Benito Mussolini who was seeded No. 1 in Italy at the time. In everything. Popularity with the crowd here means being Italian or Lew Hoad. An emotional arena where beer cans, many of them full, are often hurled at the heads of participants. Australian competitors are known to gratefully accept the barrage as a welcoming gesture. Vitas Gerulaitis once called Rome 'the asshole of the universe'.

Connors Vs Orantes. Temporarily blinded by the sun reflected from the Spaniard's teeth, Jimmy Connors fights his way bravely to the net.

Fred Perry
Mythical English tennis player whose family was so poor he had to work 15 hours a day sewing laurel wreath emblems on sportswear to pay for his coaching. Reputed to have found time to win Wimbledon three times in succession. A life-like statue of him can be seen in the BBC box at Wimbledon alongside one of Dan Maskell.

Forty love and five love down
Manuel Orantes was, as well as being two sets to love down against Vilas at the peak of his powers in the US Open. The Spaniard survived and won. Ecclesiastics in far off Madrid immediately put his name forward to the Vatican for canonization. Ion Tiriac claimed the sun reflecting from Orantes' teeth temporarily blinded his man. Vilas was moved to write a poem recording the event:
"The Iberian across the net was a slippery
little fella,
But what else, in the name of Tiriac, can come
from eating paella?
I play real good, real hard and straight —
perhaps I should be meaner,
But I'll take the loss, young bull that I am —
So don't cry for me Argentina."

Flynn, Errol
Good player but too busy to take the game seriously. Was said to have offered his body to science who unanimously rejected it.

God, what an embarrassment.

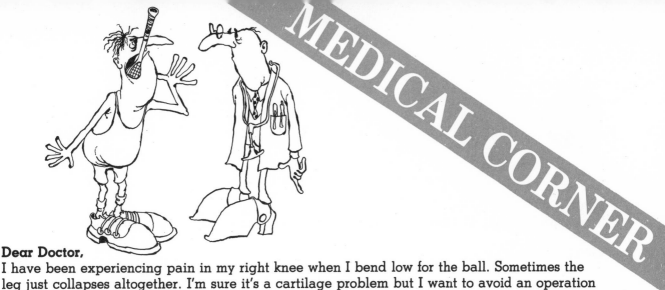

Dear Doctor,
I have been experiencing pain in my right knee when I bend low for the ball. Sometimes the leg just collapses altogether. I'm sure it's a cartilage problem but I want to avoid an operation if I can. What do you suggest?

—Mary Joint, San Francisco

Get a pregnancy test done immediately so you'll know for sure. If you feel you can't tell your parents try talking it over with your family doctor. The question of either having the child or terminating your pregnancy is really a matter for your own conscience.

Dear Doctor,
Lately whenever I toss up the ball to serve I get a very painful cramp down my back. It never occurs at any other time, and on occasions I'm left in a completely rigid position with my arm high in the air and unable to bring it down for an hour or more.

—Henry Moore, Rhode Island

You're probably tossing the ball incorrectly. Anyway, I'm a doctor, not a bloody tennis coach. Go and bother Harry Hopman.

Dear Doctor,
Is there any known cure for tennis elbow? It struck me a few months ago and although it is often quite painful I'm still able to play. It hurts the most on a running forehand drive and on the overhead backhand smash. Is there anything I can do?

—Gerry Atrick (age 94), Dayton, Ohio

Try talking about it with your wife. Bring it out into the open and discuss it freely. There is nothing anti-social about it and you most certainly will not go blind.

Dear Doctor,
I visited England in July and was privileged to play at the Wimbledon Club for six consecutive days. After some strenuous matches I suffered from double vision, hallucinations and became irritable and short tempered. What could have caused this?

—Linus Weeds, c/o Lahina Hotel, Maui, Hawaii

This phenomenon has frequently been detected by local doctors in June/July each year. Our own medical experts have determined that grass can be hazardous to your game. Prolonged exposure to the variety known as "Wimbledon Green" has affected linesmen and umpires at a local tournament there who annually suffer from identical symptoms.

Dear Doctor,
I have a severe haemorrhoid problem but I find I am unable to discuss it with anyone, including my doctor. I'm just too embarrassed to mention it. Can you help me?

No, I hate talking about things like that.

Dear Doctor,
Nearly every time I go on to play a match I get a headache. It never happens off the court. Is there anything I can do?

—J. McEnroe, New York

Try loosening your headband.
P.S. I hope your diaper rash is better.

Grob
Tennis professional. Unknown outside Sweden until he began spelling his name backwards.

Grass
Not liked by Solomon or Dibbs, but highly favoured by Paul McCartney and Mick Jagger.

Graebner, Clark
US Davis Cup player of the 1960's. Great comic entertainer and wit. Well remembered for almost thumping Ilie Nastase during the rollicking merriment of a match at London's Royal Albert Hall. Disguised as Clark Kent he was last seen in May 1974 entering a telephone booth on E 23rd St. in New York.

Gamesmanship
Little known until the recent past. Became an art form through the dedication and creative energies of a Rumanian duo in the 60's. Until then limited to stoppage of play to tighten up a shoelace or accidentally spilling a glass of Robertsons Barley Water on an opponents racquet during change of ends. Can be profitable. Has also been known to be painful: (see under Hewitt, Bob — hospital treatment following collision with a well-known British fist.)

Gut — (English & USA)
Substance used for racket stringing. May have different tensions depending on whether or not drenched by opponent with Robinsons Barley Water during change over.

Giorgio de Stefani
One of the few players who used no backhand but played forehand shots by shifting the racket from hand to hand. After doubles matches involving rapid net play he frequently required medical treatment to remove balls from his chest and stomach.

Gottfried, Brian
An outstanding doubles player as a Junior in the United States. One of the game's most dedicated players who frequently practices up to 7 hours a day. Reached a peak in his professional play in 1977 after which his game lost some of its effectiveness possibly due to a break in tournament preparation when he took 3 hours from practice to get married. Brian began his 1981 Wimbledon match preparation by reaching the semi-finals in Wimbledon 1980. One of the few players to defeat Borg 6-1 6-1. (1977 at La Costa) Proof that top players can be made, not Bjorn.

Gore, Spencer W
Won Wimbledon in 1877 before a crowd of 197. One of the first to cunningly observe that the server had an advantage. Once told a reporter, '...did you know that Mr. Jones has figured out that (at Wimbledon) 376 games have been won on serves and only 225 games on returns? Does that seem fair to you?'

Letters to the Editor

Dear Sir,

Your recent essay 'Winning — The American Way' may have shed some light on the mass psyche of tennis in the US today but it gives little hope for the eventual survival of the sport on a large scale.

'Winning' and the 'me' syndrome are little more than another sheep-like fad which must inevitably die leaving the game itself all the poorer.

If the game is to continue to grow, a quick return to the charm and humility of coming second is vital.

It is often forgotten that for one egocentric to hold the Wimbledon Singles Trophy aloft 133 players must lose. Losers were never more needed than now.

—J. Lloyd, Fort Lauderdale, Fla.

Dear Sir,

During the past few years the world's press and your own turgid pages have built up Bjorn Borg to be some sort of super-player. Let me assure you he is nothing of the sort. Regardless of what the news media tells us, history will eventually confirm his mediocrity.

To begin with, a good baseline player with an awkward and seldom used volley will never beat a natural, aggressive net player on grass. Percentages, the law of averages, call it what you will makes it mathematically impossible. Anything Borg has achieved on medium to fast surfaces so far has been nothing more than a flash in the pan.

—P. Gonzales, Los Angeles, California

Dear Sir,

I find your continuing reference to my wife contemptable and a quite uncalled for assault on her good name as a player of long service to her country.

Her dedication to the game is at least equal to that of the other great British player, Virginia Wade who, as my wife may have said will have to come to the net if she's going to beat Chrissie. Why not pick on her for a change?

I remain,
Yours sincerely,
A. Haydon-Jones (Mr.)
Tunbridge Wells, U.K.

Letters to the Editor

Dear Sirs,

I read your feature article 'Practice Makes Perfect' and I am hoping you can help me. As the wife of a touring professional I am only too aware of the heavy demands on players to maintain a high standard.

My own husband is already on the court seven or eight hours a day (leaving him little energy for anything else I might add) yet he has not won a relatively important event for two years. Lately he's been blaming his poor performances on a lack of practice due to meal breaks and sleep. I'm worried that tennis might interfere with our marriage. What should I do?

—Mrs. Gottfried, Ft. Lauderdale, Fla.

It is mediocre and insigificant little people like you who prevent those with talent from achieving greatness. An extra five or six hours' practice a day could possibly take your husband right to the top. Get off his back and stop nagging.

—Ed.

Dear Sir,

My congratulations on your superb biography of Miss Suzanne Lenglen, who I agree was probably the greatest woman player ever. It was one of the finest pieces of objective sports writing it has been my great privilege to read. However, I did pick up some minor inaccuracies which you might consider correcting for the paperback edition. The main one is the 63 page chapter on Miss Lenglen's secret love affair with the great Bill Tilden. It was common knowledge that the two players detested one another. They met only on a couple of occasions and played together just once.

Apart from counting 385 typographical errors in the article (it could happen to anyone)and seeing her birthdate given as 1919, I can only add that the score you gave for her Wimbledon singles victory (10-8, 4-6, and 9-7) of the same year was indeed correct.

Keep up the good work.

Your obedient servant,
Aubrey Bore,
Minot, Minnesota.

Mr Derk Van der Bent of Delft, Holland proudly displays his latest trophy for winning the men's singles in the Delft Closed Tournament. It was his 28th consecutive victory in an event which has been won by the Bent family every year since 1906.

*Erogenous zones of a typical
lady tennis player*

Baron Gottfried Von Cramm walks on to the court to play a practice match with King Gustav of Sweden. Gustav was forced to retire with the score at 6-1, 5-7, 13-15, 12-10, 9-9 when he broke a string in his racquet.

TENNIS TIPS ON IMPROVING YOUR GAME SERIES NO. 27

BY VITAS GERULAITIS

1. Walking onto the court

This is an essential part of the game which is often overlooked by coaches. Always be sure to open the gate first.

2. Taking balls from the can
Place your index finger through the metal ring at the end of the can marked 'top'. Pull the ring towards you until you hear a hissing sound then frown at your opponent.

3. Picking up the racquet
Forget what the purists tell you about grips; Western, Easter, Continental, etc . . . just pick the racquet so that it feels comfortable for you.

4. Checking the net
Stand one racquet vertically on the ground and place another one horizontally on top of it. The net should be roughly the same height. This exercise will require *two* racquets.

5. Playing
Hit the balls with the racquet. Preferably one ball at a time and into the court area. Your opponent should try to do the same.

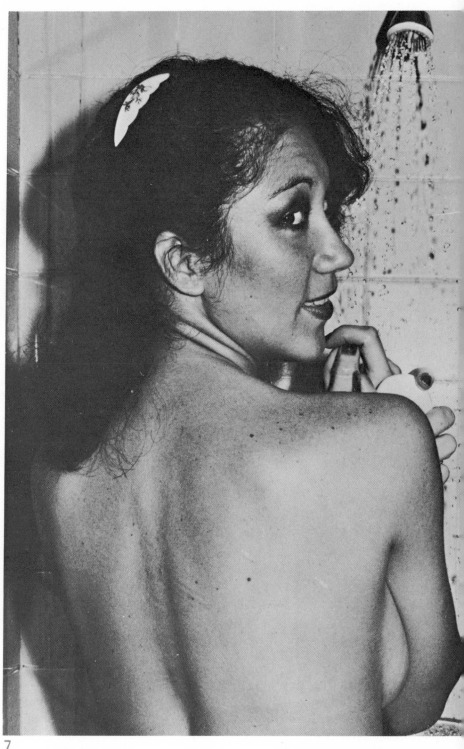

6   7

6. Walking off the court
This usually follows the game. Again, the gate should be opened before leaving.
And don't forget your balls and your racquet.

7. Taking a shower
If you're a girl, use the change-room marked 'Ladies'. Alternatively, if you are in the New York
City area, you can come to my place.

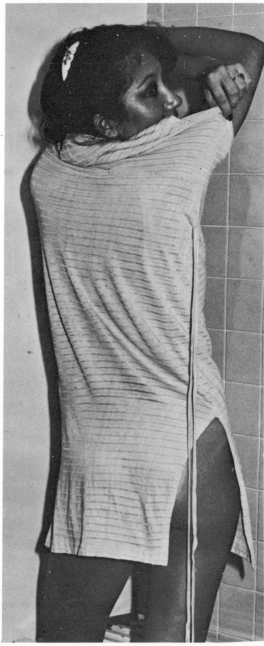

8. Getting dry
This follows a shower and you will require a towel for the purpose. If you are in the New York City area there are plenty of nice, soft towels at my place.

9. Changing
For this you will need to remove your tennis clothes and put on something suitable for a night on the town.

10. Going to a disco
For full details including how to get to my place after the disco if you happen to be in the New York City area, turn to page 101. Enjoy your game and keep your eye on the ball.

Hitler, Adolf

Once shook hands with Baron Gottfried Von Cramm. Later had the great German star thrown into jail. The Fuhrer was known to be aggressive but suffered from a backhand weakness. Served with just one ball.

Hopman, Harry

Great Australian coach of the 50's and early 60's. Made his name and no money whatsoever by monotonously winning the Davis Cup for his country year after year. To honor him in his twilight years the Australian government allowed him to go to America to work. Was last reported teaching tennis 10 hours a day in the Florida heat. Reckoned to be one of the fittest 80 year olds in the game, and needs to be.

History

What Laver made by completing the Grand Slam twice.

Hobart

Clarence Hobart played in the Wimbledon singles in 1898. He was crushed like a fly by Laurie Doherty. In an historic act of sympathy the residents of far off Tasmania's largest town renamed it in his honour. Hobart is now the cultural centre of Australia.

Hacker

Term for a low quality player. Used almost extensively by Australian Fred Stolle who has said, 'losing to a hacker hacks me off!' When he is not playing tennis Stolle is studying to become a literary giant.

Hoad, Lew

As an eleven year old Ken Rosewall played him in an exhibition match which lasted nearly two hours. Muscles won it 6-0, 6-0. Years later Hoad extracted his revenge. At Wimbledon in 1956 he borrowed fifteen shillings from the careful Rosewall and never paid it back. Hoad is thought to be hiding out in Southern Spain.

Hewitt, Bob

An expatriate Sydneysider who emigrated to South Africa in 1964. He has an outstanding doubles record in world tennis including victories in the Wimbledon men's doubles on five occasions, three times with Frew McMillan (South Africa). Has charmed umpires, linesmen and tournament officials with his warm personality and jovial approach to the game. Has been known to use his highly polished head to advantage in sunny conditions. Was once on the pain end of a well known British fist.

Henry II (English King)

Quote from 'Tennis' by G. Clerici: '. . . a modern player who often rushed the net, making himself the target of a leather ball that could hit him full in the nose, a ball stuffed with dog's hair as specified by a decree of Louix XI in 1640.' One of England's best players, Henry was the first to demonstrate the big disadvantage of attacking the net without a volley for a weapon.

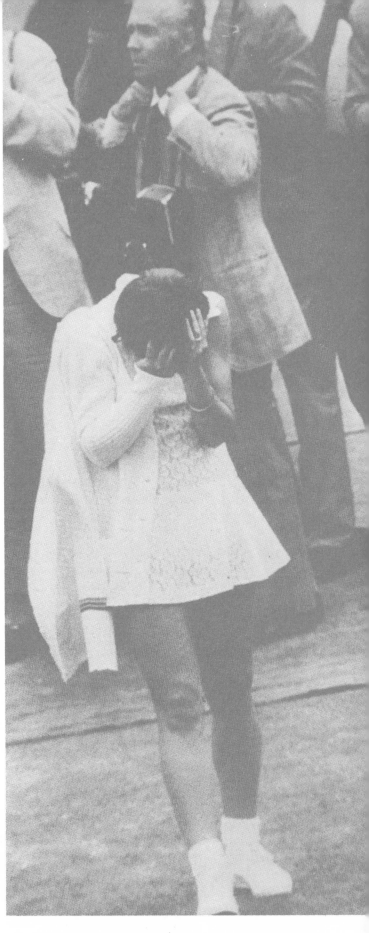

Mrs King in agony after losing concentration for a split second — but long enough for the 13½ oz racquet to fall on her head.

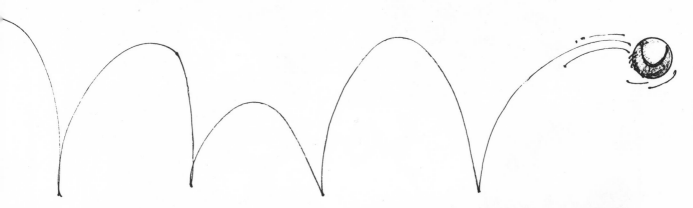

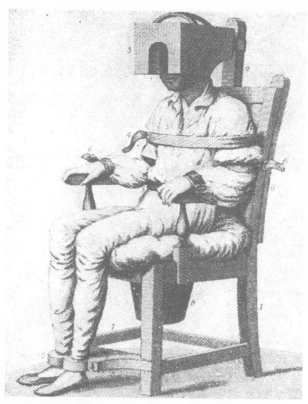

Electrical device invented by American umpire Frank Hammond which can push up to 50,000 volts through an errant linesman.

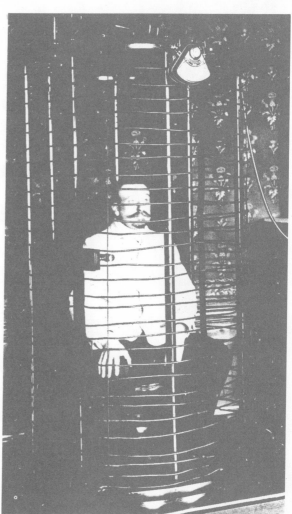

Hammond's patented protective cage. Designed for his own use at U.S. Open matches.

Hammond, Frank

Vintage umpire who was sensationally overruled by tournament officials at U.S. Open 1979 when officiating in the McEnroe/Nastase match. So offended by this autocratic interference that he relinquished the chair. Hammond is believed to be developing an electronic device for monitoring linecalls which when wired up to tournament officials can with one simple movement send 50,000 volts through a dissenter.

I

In
Judgement passed when a ball is on the line.

Ingrid Bergman
Like Bjorn Borg, Swedish.

Just Out
An opponent's call meaning just in.

Junk
A variety of slow paced balls hit to an opponent to break up his game. Ashe did it to Connors to win Wimbledon in 1975 proving once and for all who's got rhythm.

John, Elton
Played piano for Philadelphia tennis team wearing Billie Jean King's old spectacles.

Jones, Anne Haydon
Stated publicly that if Virginia is going to get back into this match she will have to come to the net.

John 'Toes' Noble
Columbus Ohio U.S.A. Has served as an umpire for over 20 years. Commonly uses shoeless tip of right middle toe to detect net balls on service. Admits to lightly sanding the end of his toe twice weekly for increased sensitivity and wears a cutaway sock for direct contact with the net. Suffered a serious whiplash injury on 2nd April 1978 during the Dayton Pro Classic when a service timed at 146 mph struck the net cord.

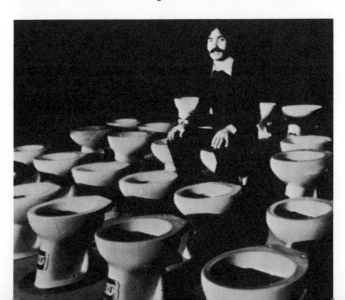

Visitor's seating, New Delhi Tennis Stadium

K

Keel
Word used by Mexican, Raul Ramirez when extremely angry.

Kent, Duke of
Husband of Duchess. Kept low profile prior to chin operation. President of All England Club. Attends Wimbledon to present silverware.

"Knock-up" (English) (Aust)
Warm up period before a match commences when players either attempt to intimidate each other by an awesome display of shots or as each disguises his actual talent by bumbling returns either out of play or into net. (U.S.A.) Has a totally different meaning.

Warming up for the much publicized "Love Doubles", the proceeds of which went to charity (except for the $360,000 which was paid to the participants).

Laver

Rodney George (Australia), born 1938. The only player to achieve the Grand Slam twice. Known as the "Rockhampton Rocket", his aggressive and spectacular style made him one of the all time greats in competitive tennis. Played with left hand attached to a forearm measuring 22 inches in circumference; this proportionately should have given Laver a height of 8' 2½".

Laycold
Night out with Russian female tennis player. Also describes a particular playing surface.

Election of the President of the Linesman's Association

Linesman
A deaf and blind person who sits in a chair on the court to mark the position of various lines.

Lox
Equipment fitted to Tel Aviv tennis changing rooms to deter players from petty crime.

Larnerd, William
In 1896 he amazed Wimbledon by winning the first two sets from Herbert Baddeley in the final. His luck went sour when some strings broke in his only racquet. Geneologists have suggested Larnerd had connections with the Rosewall family in Sydney, Australia.

McGregor, Ken

Aussie Davis Cup star of the 50's. Partnered Sedgman. Retired at the peak of his career to play and coach Australian Rules Football. Although this game is virtually unheard of outside Australia, many keen supporters of the spine-wrenching activity strongly contend that if the Australian island continent was joined to the US and European land masses, then their game would take over from soccer as the world's biggest spectator sport.

McMillan,   Frew (South Africa)

Shares a distinguished Doubles record with Bob Hewitt. Wears a white peaked cap during play to deflect sunlight shining from partner's head. Hits double handed backhand and forehand. Is believed to be experimenting with double handed service but is yet to overcome problems with service toss-up.

Mottram Christopher (Buster)

Top ranked British player with a distinguished Davis Cup record. A determined and agile player despite size 13 shoes. Doubles with Enoch Powell and stands slightly to his partner's right.

A PRACTICAL GUIDE TO MATCH PLAY FOR THE CLUB PLAYER

Volumes have been written about the psychological approach to tennis.
Pre-match training, diet, calisthenics; the physical and emotional preparation required
to condition top players and sustain them through the pressures of competitive tennis.
Overlooked in most tennis texts are the practical aids which can shift the balance in
tight matches and ensure victory for club players.
Recent research and study of the 'average' game are detailed below, and should prove
invaluable to players of club standard:
Having warmed up secretly for at least half an hour,

a) Always arrive at the club late. Not to the extent that
   you are disqualified, but be sufficiently tardy as to
   raise your already tense opponent's hopes of being
   awarded a walkover. Rush onto the court half dressed
   and, if possible, smoking.

b) Continue to smoke during the hit up, and, if you have more than one racquet change continually during both the hit up and the match. Tap the strings and comment loudly about tension and humidity, which should increase your opponent's. During the pre-game knock, hit all balls out or into the net.

c) Inspect your opponent's racquet either before the match commences or at change over breaks. If any string appears worn — tell him. Offer the use of your spare 'when that string goes'. Given the opportunity to test your opponent's string tension tell him they are either sloppy or too taut.

d) Should you win the toss make your opponent serve. Joke about needing an 'early break'. In the absence of an umpire call *all* faults loudly.

e) Talk constantly during the change over about anything to anyone including the umpire, your opponent and any spectators. If your opponent objects apologise for breaking his concentration.

f) To prevent your opponent from settling into his service rhythm wipe spectacles, drop a contact lens, adjust athletic support or retie shoelaces as he tosses the ball to serve. On vital points (if possible) break wind loudly and apologise profusely.

g) On your own service bounce the ball repeatedly; toss the ball to the extreme right or left and abort your service action. Occasionally bounce the ball on your shoe and then retrieve it, apologetically.

h) 'Forget' the score; to assist your opponent in recalling the correct score verbally replay each point. 'You served to my backhand, I hit a short chip to the forehand court, you ran in, hit a cross court to my forehand, I lobbed, you ran back, retrieved it and hit a forehand to me at net, I volleyed it away for a winner.' By the time this proceeds through to 30-40 your opponent should be well on the way to a complete emotional collapse.

i) If these tactics have not affected your opponent's game and he is still able to hit shots which are beating you, compliment him on change over on his unusual and 'natural' game. e.g. 'You have no follow through on that forehand, but what power'. 'Volley control with that backswing is unbelievable', etc. It all helps.

j) Look for the signs of your opponent cracking. Glazed eyes and pulsing temples are sure signs.

k) The coup de grace to ensure victory comes when your opponent's game finally goes to water. Once he starts overhitting, double faulting and hitting the bottom of the net regularly, offer assistance 'slow down and watch the ball', 'head down', 'get side on', etc. One most effective device is the 'get your racquet back early' routine, especially in the case of a suspect backhand.

Players in moments of severe stress have been known to freeze in the racquet back position.

Always jump the net to ensure that any gallery is aware of the result.

The use of these pointers will add to your enjoyment and success in the game at club level.

And remember: The most important thing is not to win but to take part; just as the most important thing in life is not the triumph but the struggle. The essential thing is to have fought well.

... AWW STOP BITCHING LADY, YOU CAN PLAY TENNIS ANYTIME!

Net
The amount left after a player has paid his expenses.

Nastase
Even-tempered and loveable Rumanian star who was hounded throughout his career by psychotic umpires, linesmen, ballboys, photographers and spectators. Invited to Borg's wedding.

Net cord judge
Sleeping official who has acute sensitivity in right forefinger.

Okker
Australian term for friend.

Passing shot
Nasty comment made as opponents change ends.

Piles
Ken Rosewall is reckoned to have piles, according to sources at the Bank of New South Wales head office in Sydney who have seen his savings deposit book.

Percentage tennis
Traditionally, the way to win matches BBB (Before Bjorn Borg). Following Roscoe Tanner's epic Wimbledon final against the Swede in 1979, Tanner was quoted as saying, 'You can't beat Borg by playing percentage tennis'. Mr. Tanner was last reported to be entering a monastery.

Poacher
Player who encroaches onto partner's side of net intent on keeping all the game to himself. Some players poach without licence or partner's approval. If the game ends in defeat a poacher is immersed in boiling water for 2-3 minutes.

Pim
Dr. Joshua (1889-1942) an Irish competitor who played with such uncanny accuracy that it was once said of him that he could hit a coin placed anywhere on the court. On tour in his twilight years in Sydney Australia on June 11th 1940 he was persuaded to give an exhibition of this unusual skill. The demonstration was thwarted when a six year old boy named Kenny ran onto the court, picked up the coin and disappeared in a nearby branch of the Bank of New South Wales.

Pressroom
A smoke filled room on the tournament site generously littered with old sandwich crusts and empty beer cans. A special pass is needed to gain entry. At British and Australian events proof of intoxication must be shown at the door.

GREAT MATCHES SERIES

No. 296

One hard-bitten sports writer called it 'a war of attrition'. Off the court Connors and McEnroe have little time for each other. Some say hate is more appropriate. Many observers of their bitter contest at Wimbledon in 1980 rate the match as more electric than the dramatic final itself. The game was gruelling, grunting, bruising and angry. Niceties were non-existent: it was war, pure and simple.

The World's Best Tennis Book Ever was at Centre Court to record the epic battle on film. Turn to page 34 for a pull-out souvenir photo of this great match which ended in a victory for McEnroe at 6-3, 3-6, 6-4, 6-3.

Nastase puts himself and his opponent to sleep during an attempt on the 1982 'Argue With an Official' record presently held by J. McEnroe of the U.S.A. Shortly after this photo was taken the umpire also nodded off and fell out of his chair.

TOP TENNIS: A LOOK BEHIND THE SCENES

The World's Best Tennis Book Ever takes you behind the scenes at Wimbledon.

The scene: the ladies changing room at the All-England Club, Wimbledon. It's the second week of the championships and the air is tense and a little dank. Virginia Wade enters, ducking under some wet frilly knickers strung between the lockers. Her quarter final match has just ended, she looks drained, exhausted. Cries from the English partisans in the crowd can still be heard coming from the Centre Court. But it is unlikely to do any good; Navratilova will probably not want to play the match again. Virginia slumps onto a bench in the corner and drops her Maxplys. Meanwhile, at the other end of the room, Martina wipes a small bead of perspiration from her brow and begins some press ups.

"One, two, three, four..."

There's a loud crash from the side door, people shouting.

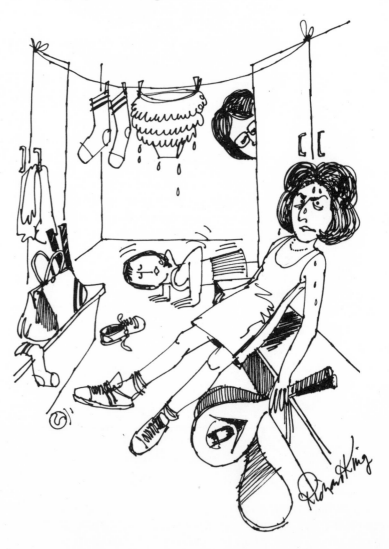

"No John, you can't come in . . . I know you got knocked out in the first round, but that's not my goddamned fault. We beat the Borgs at doubles didn't we? No, go away. I'll see you after I've finished with Goolagong."

The door slams shut. Chrissie Evert walks in removing her track suit.

"Hi Ginny! How'd it go?"

Ginny: *"Piss off. You know bloody well how it went."*
Chris: *"Well, at least you retain your femininity and charm. She (whispers) plays like a man. These East Europeans don't become more feminine just by moving to America."*
Ginny: (grimacing, fists clenched)   *"I had her 5-3 in the second set and I blew it."*
Chris: *"Maybe you should have gone to the net and pressured her. Anyways, that's what Ann Jones said in the commentary."*
Ginny: *"Bugger Ann Jones. I've been number one in Britain a bloody sight longer than she has."*

(Loud grunts continue from Navratilova's end of the room . . . *"99, 100, 101, 102 . . ."*)

Ginny: *"Who are you playing, Goolagong?"*
Chris: *"Yes. I find her a bit sugary, don't you. I mean she's all right but that husband of hers is a bit corny and he smokes all the time too.*
           "Poor John was sitting next to him in the players box last year and he spent the next four days coughing. I think it probably affected his game."

The door opens and Billie Jean King enters.

Billie: *"We're on in three minutes Martina."*
Martina: *". . . 121, 122, yeah, ok, I'll be with you . . . 123, 124 . . ."*
Billie: *"We're playing Casals and Stove we need to attack serve more than we've been doing try short angles returns to the backhand side and lob Casals like crazy Rosie's a good friend but she's a short-ass and we need to exploit that and keep the ball off Betty's forehand I know she looks clumsy but she's quite agile on that side of her body and . . ."*

     ". . . 151, 152, 153 . . ."

Ginny: *"You'd think B.J. would have had enough tennis by now. I mean, that knee bandage she wears looks terrible. I think I'd rather stop playing altogether than wear one of those things."*
Chris: *"That's exactly what John said to me. He said that if I ever have to wear a knee bandage he'd make me stop playing. Well, so I asked him just how we would eat and pay the mortgage if I stopped playing. It would have been different with Jimmy of course, he may not be as hot as he was but at least he has a regular income."*

     ". . . 166, 167, 168 . . ."

The main door opens and a large bosom appears. Behind it is BBC Radio reporter Ann Jones, beaming, tape recorder and microphone at the ready.

A. Jones: *"Well Ginny, that was jolly bad luck. I thought you were in control at 5-3 in the second set. Could you tell us what happened?"*
Ginny: *"I started to get a bit tense and I was pushing the ball instead of hitting it."*
A. Jones: *"Both Dan Maskell and I felt you changed your tactics at that point too. You were staying back more and playing Martina from the baseline."*

     ". . . 198, 199, 200, 201 . . ."

Billie: (screaming) *"For Chrissake Martina we're due on the court . . ."*
Ginny: *"She was passing me too much when I moved forward."*
A. Jones: *"Don't you think you would have pressured her more by coming to the net?"*
Ginny: *"Piss off! I'm not number one in Britain for nothing!"*

     ". . . 221, 222, 223 . . ."

— ends —

(1) FOREHAND DELIVERY

The 'Ready' position — face on with racquet in front of body.

Take an extended backswing. Cock handle slightly (Never vice versa).

Shift weight to front foot as swing commences.

Face target in the ready position — side on with the racquet held in front of body.

With weight on back foot commence backswing with racquet moving to "backscratch position".

Swing forward and up transferring weight to front foot.

'THROWING THE RACQUET'

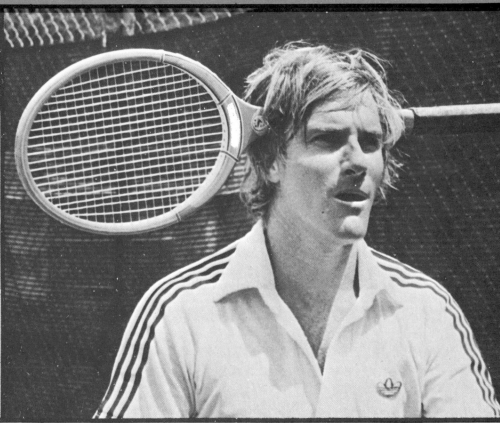

When wrist and arm are in a straight line release the racquet smoothly by opening hand.

(2) SERVICE OR OVERHEAD DELIVERY

Straighten arm with a wrist snap and release racquet which will move in a curved trajectory to target.

Queue

Line of spectators seeking entry to tournament; *"Far queue"*, a term sometimes directed at tournament officials who decline to reverse bad linecalls.

Qualifier

A series of preliminary matches between players whose computer ranking does not give them direct entry to a tournament. Players compete on a 'knockout' elimination basis for a limited number of places in the draw. Albert Squint, a 42 year old Queensland professional, has the distinction of never proceeding past the first round in 192 qualifiers played over 26 years as a touring pro. He has, in that time, used the same racket and tennis shoes without either restring or retread. "They just don't seem to wear out", he said. He recalls his longest rally as being three shots, all serves including a netcord. He currently receives financial assistance from the Combined Queensland Septic Tank Associations. Their motto, "We know our business, we've been in it for years", seems appropriate.

Riggs, Robert Larimore
Defeated 6-0, 6-1 by Baron Gottfried von Cramm at Queen's Club in 1939, and that year Riggs went on to win 3 Wimbledon titles. He practised continually, building his game to a peak for his 6-4, 6-3, 6-3 defeat by Billie Jean King at the Houston Astrodome one evening in 1973. Later that night he pulled a hamstring while carrying out a load of banknotes from a Houston bookmaker.

Rob
A ball hit high over an opponent's head by a Chinese player.

Reprimand
A short talking to, given by some players to the umpire.

Rally
Hitting the ball back and forth across the net. Also seen in Germany 1938-45.

Ruffles
Caused a sensation at sedate Wimbledon in 1954 when seen on outside of ladies panties.

Ruffels, Ray
Caused a sensation at sedate Wimbledon in 1974 when seen on inside of ladies panties.

Slow Clay
Mohammad Ali, aged 93.

Sponsorship
Money given by Ilie Nastase to support the International Tennis Federation.

Slice
Percentage taken by managers.

Stilwell, Graham
Who?

Shakespeare, William
'. . .When we have match'd our rackets to these balls,
We will in France, by God's grace, play a set.'
        Act I, Henry V
N.B. A French title eluded both Henry and Shakespeare.

String Orchestra
The sound coming from coach Lennart Bergelin's hotel bedroom late at night as Borg's 84lb tension gut part company from their frames. This is a fact and well known amongst players on the circuit. It is interesting to note that no 'pinging' has been heard from Borg's quarters.

Stance
Position of body prior to playing shot. A play or device used by players at after-match functions, as in "Let's stance".

Spin
A method of stroke play which induces a pronounced rolling of the ball in the air either sideways, forwards or backwards depending on whether the racquet face moves respectively across, over or under the ball. Sometimes relates to older players who have lost their touch e.g. "has spin".

*Ashe and Noah (doubles) during a power failure at
an evening match at Flushing Meadow.*

Tank
Place where officials look for players who should have won easily but instead lose convincingly. Use of this term not approved by A.T.P.

Topspin
Balls rotate forward after being hit. Frequently occurs in doubles when errant server strikes net partner with cannonball first serve. Medical treatment usually required.

Technique
Englishman Roger Taylor's was reputed to be excellent. Gerulaitis' was even better.

Tennis Camp
Gay player from San Francisco.

Team Tennis
Disastrous attempt to fill empty US stadiums with bloodthirsty out-of-season football fans. Now happily defunct.

Umpire
Official who keeps score during match. Duties include provoking players by confirming bad linecalls.

Underspin
A backward rotation of balls after shot. Can cause permanent damage unless given immediate treatment.

Underarm (U.S.A.)
Racquet strikes ball in an upward looped fashion without racquet reaching over shoulder level. **(Italian)** defies description.

Unreturnable
Single finger gesture made by Nastase to the Royal Box at Wimbleton.

Vitas Gerulaitis
A top U.S. professional regarded as one of the quickest players in the game. Plays best under strobe lighting.

Windsor, Elizabeth Regina
Housewife, mother and Queen of England. Gets free tickets to Wimbledon but only attends in Centenary years.

Wagner, Richard
Expelled from German Davis Cup squad for playing loud music in motel room after lights out.

Wives
Sometimes travel on the circuit so their husbands won't be bored when not playing matches, practicing, drinking with friends, sightseeing, being lavishly entertained by wealthy divorcees or groped by hordes of enthusiastic young and beautiful women.

Wilson
One time British policitian. Seeded No. 1 for the House of Commons in the 60's and 70's.

Winner
A shot which beats an opponent. A player who hits sufficient winners usually is one. Consistent winners can be recognised by massive muscular development of the forearm hand from habitually collecting prize money.

Israeli official Mr Samuel Bagel photographed in the players lounge at the Israel Open following a disputed dominos game with Illie Nastase

And now...

The German Page

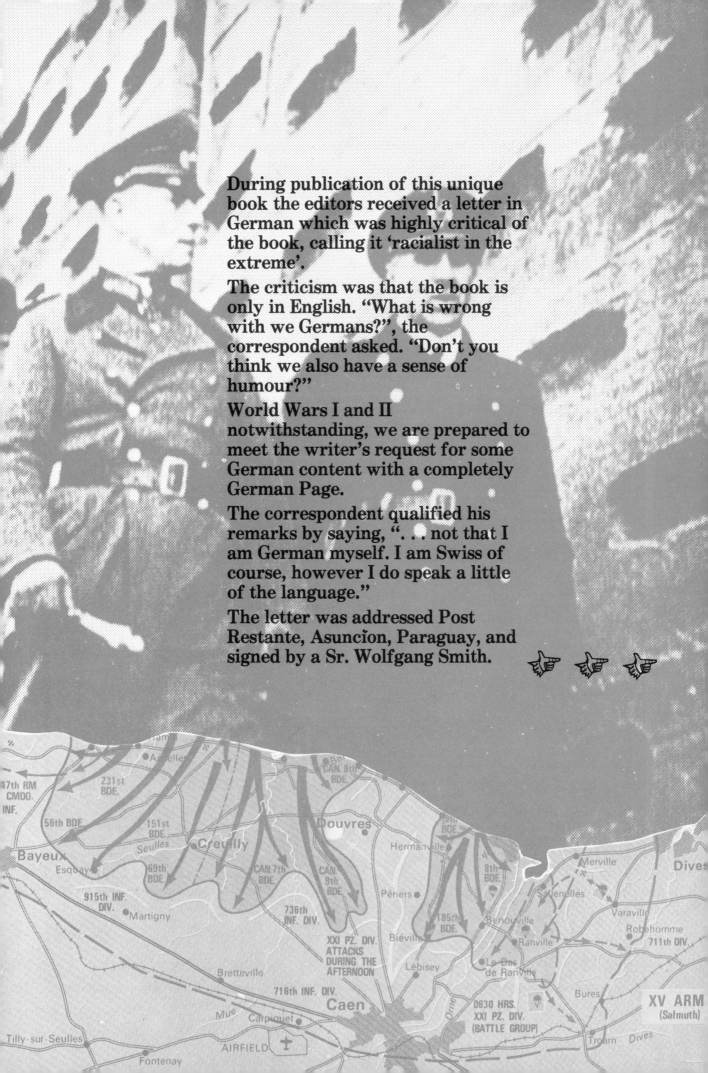

During publication of this unique book the editors received a letter in German which was highly critical of the book, calling it 'racialist in the extreme'.

The criticism was that the book is only in English. "What is wrong with we Germans?", the correspondent asked. "Don't you think we also have a sense of humour?"

World Wars I and II notwithstanding, we are prepared to meet the writer's request for some German content with a completely German Page.

The correspondent qualified his remarks by saying, ". . . not that I am German myself. I am Swiss of course, however I do speak a little of the language."

The letter was addressed Post Restante, Asuncion, Paraguay, and signed by a Sr. Wolfgang Smith.

Willenskraft/Energie

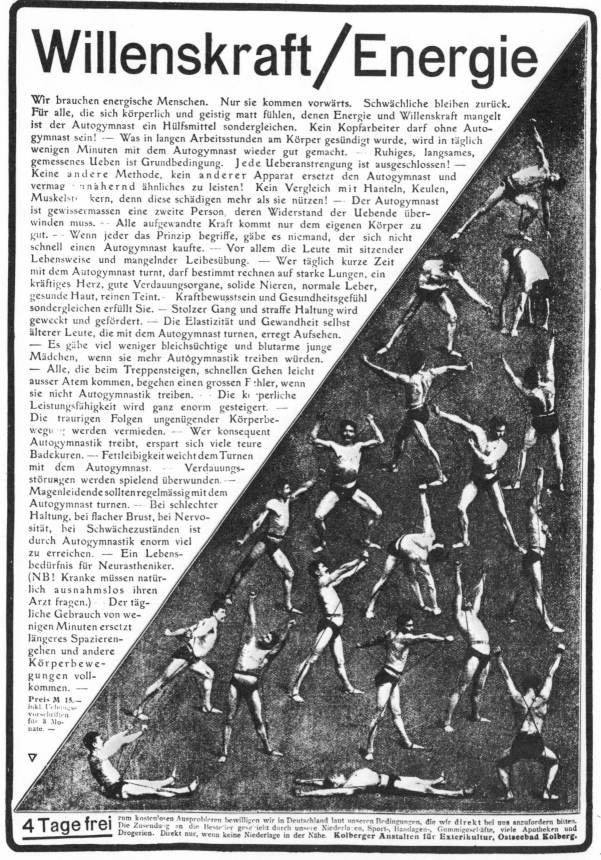

Wir brauchen energische Menschen. Nur sie kommen vorwärts. Schwächliche bleiben zurück. Für alle, die sich körperlich und geistig matt fühlen, denen Energie und Willenskraft mangelt ist der Autogymnast ein Hülfsmittel sondergleichen. Kein Kopfarbeiter darf ohne Autogymnast sein! — Was in langen Arbeitsstunden am Körper gesündigt wurde, wird in täglich wenigen Minuten mit dem Autogymnast wieder gut gemacht. — Ruhiges, langsames, gemessenes Ueben ist Grundbedingung. Jede Ueberanstrengung ist ausgeschlossen! — Keine andere Methode, kein anderer Apparat ersetzt den Autogymnast und vermag annähernd ähnliches zu leisten! Kein Vergleich mit Hanteln, Keulen, Muskelstärkern, denn diese schädigen mehr als sie nützen! — Der Autogymnast ist gewissermassen eine zweite Person, deren Widerstand der Uebende überwinden muss. — Alle aufgewandte Kraft kommt nur dem eigenen Körper zu gut. — Wenn jeder das Prinzip begriffe, gäbe es niemand, der sich nicht schnell einen Autogymnast kaufte. — Vor allem die Leute mit sitzender Lebensweise und mangelnder Leibesübung. — Wer täglich kurze Zeit mit dem Autogymnast turnt, darf bestimmt rechnen auf starke Lungen, ein kräftiges Herz, gute Verdauungsorgane, solide Nieren, normale Leber, gesunde Haut, reinen Teint. — Kraftbewusstsein und Gesundheitsgefühl sondergleichen erfüllt Sie. — Stolzer Gang und straffe Haltung wird geweckt und gefördert. — Die Elastizität und Gewandheit selbst älterer Leute, die mit dem Autogymnast turnen, erregt Aufsehen. — Es gäbe viel weniger bleichsüchtige und blutarme junge Mädchen, wenn sie mehr Autogymnastik treiben würden. — Alle, die beim Treppensteigen, schnellen Gehen leicht ausser Atem kommen, begehen einen grossen Fehler, wenn sie nicht Autogymnastik treiben. — Die körperliche Leistungsfähigkeit wird ganz enorm gesteigert. — Die traurigen Folgen ungenügender Körperbewegung werden vermieden. — Wer konsequent Autogymnastik treibt, erspart sich viele teure Badekuren. — Fettleibigkeit weicht dem Turnen mit dem Autogymnast. — Verdauungsstörungen werden spielend überwunden. — Magenleidende sollten regelmässig mit dem Autogymnast turnen. — Bei schlechter Haltung, bei flacher Brust, bei Nervosität, bei Schwächezuständen ist durch Autogymnastik enorm viel zu erreichen. — Ein Lebensbedürfnis für Neurastheniker. (NB! Kranke müssen natürlich ausnahmslos ihren Arzt fragen.) — Der tägliche Gebrauch von wenigen Minuten ersetzt längeres Spazierengehen und andere Körperbewegungen vollkommen.

Preis M 15.—
inkl. Uebungsvorschriften für 3 Monate. —

THE PEOPLES
TENNIS
FEDERATION
OF THE U.S.S.R

To the editors,
The World's Best Tennis Book Ever

Dear Sirs,

Perhaps you have forgotten, but it was acts of intimidation similar to that of your German complainant that began the last World War. For the media to bow to such heinous pressure is to ask for trouble.

By inserting a German Page in your book you have unwittingly sown the seeds of War in Europe. That much is obvious. Ultimately such acts of open aggression against the peace-loving people of Russia must end in the destruction of your so-called democracy and free press.

Unless the German Page is removed and a page given to the Union of Soviet Socialist Republics and each of its satellite states, including Cuba, we will immediately halt all sales of your humourless work throughout the Eastern Bloc.

Yours sincerely,

V. Piztof

Cd. Vladimir Piztof
Committee Chairman

Cnr. Jenin Hwy & Elm St., Omsk 2059, U.S.S.R.

Xerophite
Able to endure a long drought.
(See under Lloyd, J. and Scanlon, W.)

The J. McEnroe Memorial Troph

Yvon Petra
French player who won Wimbledon in 1946. Should appear under 'P' listing but editor short on Y's.

Zadrobsky, J
Czechoslavakian Davis Cup player and team mate of Drobny. Like Drobny he defected to the West around 1948. Went so far West was never heard of again.

The Elwood Dirge
Home for the Elderly.
White Mountains,
New Hampshire
U S A

Dear Mr Riggs,
                You were a very young man
when I first saw you play, and although I
had seen many great players I thought you
were going to be the best.
        It was at Wimbeldon in 1939 and you
won all three titles and a lot of money
from the bookmakers. After the singles final
I managed to get your autograph on the
back of my program. Would you believe, I
have kept it all these years? Your
signature is among my proudest possessions.
        But could you let me have my pen back?
It was a gold Parker and of great sentimental
value.

                Yours Sincerely,
                Mrs Doris Trumbuck.

FRAMES OF YESTERYEAR

A number of great innovative ideas in tennis frames have appeared over the years only to disappear due to the vested interests of big manufacturers. Here are some of the more successful ones.

Cast Iron
The lightweight version of this racquet first appeared in 1908 in Northern England. It weighed 21 lbs. It was used with tremendous success by Yorkshire County player T.W. 'Big Tom' Pratt who ruptured himself picking up half a dozen of the newly-strung frames from his local sports shop.
Disadvantages: Very brittle, easily broken.

Rhinocerous Horn
Believed in the East to have aphrodisiac qualities. Six of these were produced in 1925 for the China Davis Cup Team who ate them before the final singles match could be played.
Disadvantages: None, if you're married to a Chinese Davis Cup player.

Glass
Developed in Waterford by Irish international Mick McBride, it was very expensive, easily broken and McBride had it made in an attempt to stop himself throwing his racquet. It worked, enabling him to keep cool long enough to win the Co. Cork Closed title in 1951. Unhappily the frame shattered when McBride tapped the umpire on the knee in the perfunctory gesture of thanks which followed his victory. Artery severed, the man bled to death where he sat.
Disadvantages: Expensive.

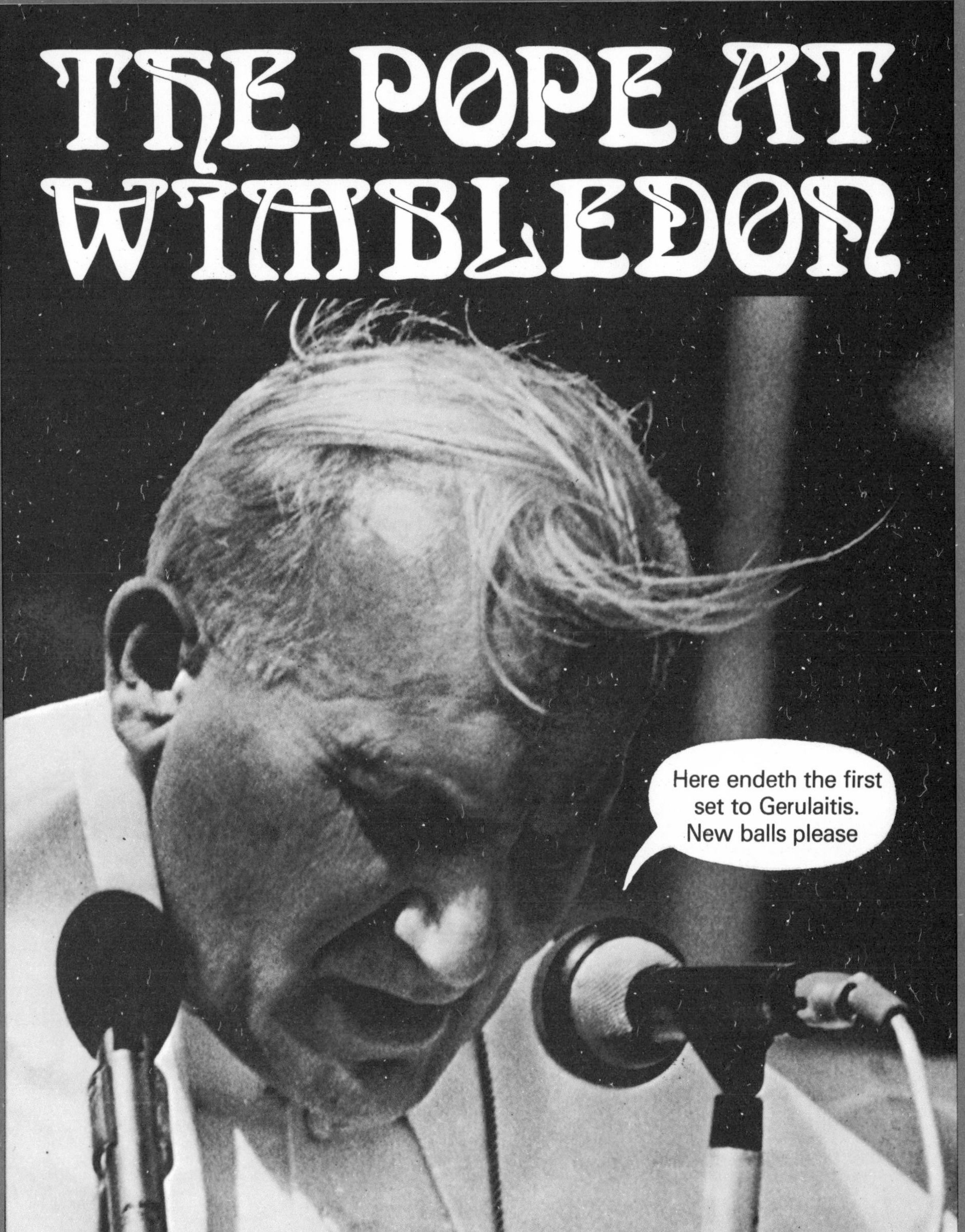
THE POPE AT WIMBLEDON
Here endeth the first set to Gerulaitis. New balls please

Pope John Paul II, the most travelled Papal Leader in history, was invited to officiate at Wimbledon's famous centre court. For a few hours His Holiness took the umpire's chair and checked line calls.

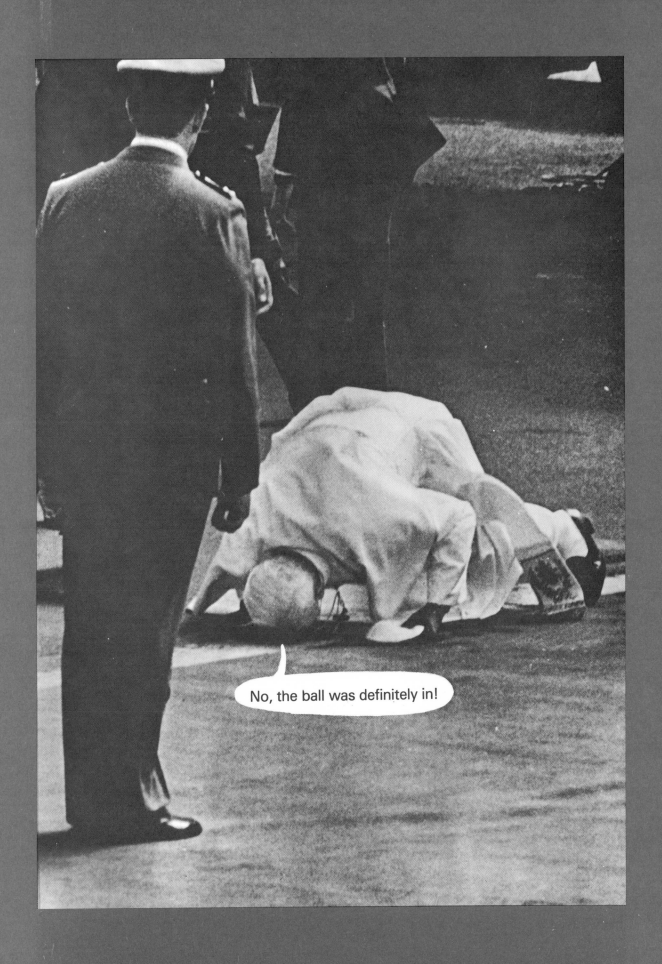

THE MAGIC OF WIMBLEDON

These rare photographs show Billie Jean King, Illie Nastase and Bill Scanlon performing levitation at Wimbledon. This is not a unique gift among players on the circuit. Nastase has even been known to raise officials to a standing position simply by projecting his index finger upwards.

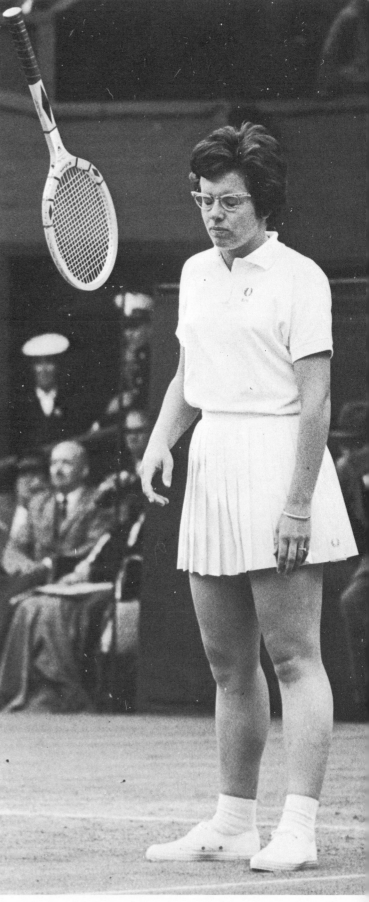

死生定

近接力實戰

門劇有料逢

打和要射十二碼

七百卅萬美元

中國「金杯牌」足球 國際比賽中可使用

中國獲准重返 國際手球聯會

波格反手聖球堪稱絕技 觀衆大喊觀止值回票價

兩場腰斬賽事 維持比賽結果

十月份觀衆減 收入增

徐實生稱中國正提高網球水平

波格願到中國任教

有關方面明日研究波格再度訪華日期

訪

The World's Best Tennis Book Ever Centrefold Girl

Fold here

Annie

Measurements:	*38" — 25" — 35"*
Born:	*1964 England — Little Snoring.*
Favourite pastimes:	*Stone rubbings, Byzantian church music, tapestry weaving.*
Ambitions:	*Just to be a nice girl that everybody likes, and to marry Mr. Fredrick Stone my fiance.*
Favourite clothes:	*Tennis things, cut offs and black leather things.*
Turn ons:	*Wind in my hair, baked beans.*
Turn offs:	*Mr. Ernest Byzantian our church organist who is a perverted person.*

COURT ETIQUETTE SERIES No. 22
By Illie Nastase

EVONNE TAKES A SENTIMENTAL JOURNEY

Sixteen years ago a pretty 12 year old part-aboriginal girl was discovered playing tennis in the small outback town of Barrellan, NSW, Australia.

Seven years later, Evonne won the Women's Singles title at Wimbledon and repeated the feat in 1980. Now a household name, Evonne Household-Cawley recently returned to her home town for a short visit.

Following weeks of negotiations, the publishers have purchased the one-time only rights to the photos taken by Evonne on her return to her home town as a celebrity.

The old tennis clubhouse

Lunchtime crowds downtown.

The new swimming centre and leisure complex.

Looking across Gum Tree Crescent to our neighbours' house.

A prize-winning canine goes through his paces at the annual dog show.

The recently completed Goolagong Expressway slices through the suburban sprawl.

A view of the Botanical Gardens.

The bustling town centre.

The new, modern drive-in cinema.

Members of the local chamber orchestra share a quiet moment on the patio of the arts centre.

The house where I was born — now beautifully renovated it is permanently preserved as an important historical building.

Public Apology to John Newcombe

The editors wish to apologise to John Newcombe for failing to include his name in this great work. As a player and a champion John has done much for the game of tennis. His powerful style, his sportsmanlike manner both on and off the court and his willingness to put something back into a sport from which he has gained so much, has endeared him to millions of tennis enthusiasts the world over.

Now, as a successful businessman and entrepreneur John Newcombe is displaying the same wit and flair which made him so famous in the tennis arenas of the world.

It is indeed with heartfelt sincerity that we apologise to you Newk. Your charisma and charm both on and off the court has done so very much to promote tennis and to make it one of the most popular sports in the world today.

Personalities of the stature of John Newcombe are rare in the world at large. In tennis the 'Newks' of the world are few and far between. Today John Newcombe is a household name. His own brand of sports clothes with the familiar one-eye and moustache are known to people in every country and from every walk of life. A family man with simple tastes John Newcombe is a credit to Australia and to the game of tennis. Children could do little better than to follow his fine example both on and off the court.

We really do apologise for leaving out of our book this great name in tennis who is an idol to millions of children all over the world, both on and off the court.

Today, John Newcombe *is* tennis. His tennis camps are known to players all over the world and his constant efforts to help juniors to develop have not gone unnoticed. Both on and off the court Newk has won the respect and applause of the tennis public, and we apologise for leaving him out.

There is not a tennis book published in recent times which does not give due space to this great champion. So we hope you will accept this apology Newk. We really mean it and at the same time we would like to apologise to Ken Rosewall who is at this very moment at home in Pymble writing out a writ. Pymble is not far from your place in Sydney, John, so maybe you could run over there and show Kenny this apology. You might even have a workout with him while you're there — if he's going to play in the Grand Masters Series he'll need to work on his serve. There is no way he will get to the top with a weak serve like that.

Anyway, Newk, once again our apologies for leaving you out.

All the very best.

Yours sincerely,

The Publishers.

P.S. Any chance of a discount on Lotto shirts?

Linesman of the Year Award